Lucy H. Yates

A Handbook of Fish Cookery

Outlook

Lucy H. Yates

A Handbook of Fish Cookery

1. Auflage | ISBN: 978-3-73261-877-4

Erscheinungsort: Paderborn, Deutschland

Erscheinungsjahr: 2018

Outlook Verlag GmbH, Paderborn.

Lucy H. Yates

A Handbook of Fish Cookery

Outlook

A HANDBOOK

OF

FISH COOKERY

HOW TO BUY, DRESS, COOK, AND EAT FISH

BY

LUCY H. YATES

Author of "The Profession of Cookery from a French Point of View."

LONDON

WARD, LOCK & CO., LIMITED

WARWICK HOUSE, SALISBURY SQUARE, E.C.
NEW YORK AND MELBOURNE
1897

INTRODUCTION.

In spite of a considerable amount of trade grumbling, the best part of the market is still held by English fish, as a glance at any time over the names on the crates will show. The foreign importations, though large, are not nearly so extensive as might be supposed.

As a rule the north British ports furnish the largest supply; the southern ports suffer the most from foreign competition. Continental freightage also is light, and as the foreigner rarely keeps very closely to the laws of "fence months," he gets fish into the market when no home-caught of the same kind is to be had.

If all people, both rich and poor, could be persuaded to eat fish more freely, they would be benefited both in health and pocket.

If the *demand* were greater the *supply* would be more liberal, more varied, and also much cheaper.

At present, although there is much complaining about catches falling off, many grounds yielding but a poor harvest, yet tons of fish are annually sent away from the markets for manure.

The trade is both risky and variable, consequently prices have to be kept up that the dealer may realise some profit, and for this state of things *the modern housewife is largely accountable.*

It is not wholly a question of price, although there is still much to desire on this point.

Ignorance, especially with the working-man's wife, will generally be found to be the cause of the aversion which many housewives have to the cooking of fish; even in middle and upper class households much ignorance as to the kinds of fish and the best means of making use of them prevails.

The poorer classes still regard fish as "nothing to make a meal of," and, sad to say, a great many of the poor of our cities will not eat fish, however cheaply they may get it. They have many advantages of getting it which those who live in superior neighbourhoods have not.

Often before the Central Market closes, first-rate cod is to be had for twopence the pound—a seven-pound cod for a shilling. Plentiful and wholesome as cod is, it is seldom much thought of by poor people. Salted, sun-dried cod, is thought beneath notice, although large quantities are consumed on the continent, and some very dainty dishes made therefrom.

Plaice, too, generally to be had at fourpence the pound, is but lightly esteemed.

Humble Londoners care most for smoked fish, "something that has a grip with it," they say. To meet this demand many adulterations are practised by the cockney curer. "Haddocks" are often but indifferent codling. The "Finnan Haddie" was caught in the Scheldt, and Stavanger herrings are passed off as Yarmouth bloaters.

Unwholesome common lobsters, winkles, and whelks, are preferred to good substantial fish, and, as before stated, ignorance of the proper methods of cooking is most frequently the reason of this.

Where late dinners, with people of small incomes, are coming more into favour, it is found an economy, as it is also considered the "correct thing," to have a course of fish. Indeed, as an economical article of diet, fish has few rivals.

Many people who really would enjoy eating it are debarred from doing so by its being invariably badly cooked, or presented always in the same monotonous dress.

Phosphorus being essential for brain food, and as analysis has proved fish to contain a greater amount than almost any other article of diet, it is the more valuable still on this account.

The fish which afford the most nourishment are the kinds which most resemble meat, as salmon, mackerel, &c.; turbot and halibut, though strictly belonging to the "lighter" order, are very nourishing on account of the amount of meat which they bear in proportion to bone. The whiter kinds of fish are the most easily digestible, as soles or cod, whiting, &c., and some kinds of river fish, notably perch.

With the exception of trout—and perhaps pike—fresh-water fish are less esteemed than they deserve to be.

Salmon is sometimes called a river fish, though genuinely it is not so, as, although born in the river, the sea is its home and natural sphere.

In Parisian restaurants many dainty dishes are prepared from fish caught in the Seine; and in country places where sea-water fish is often difficult to obtain, the ponds and rivers will often furnish excellent substitutes.

All fresh-water fish—with the exception of trout—is at its best in winter-time.

Shell-fish, perfectly harmless in themselves as they may be, exemplify the saying that "what is one man's meat is another man's poison;" accordingly, where they are found to disagree they should be strictly avoided.

Oysters, the most highly esteemed of shell-fish, are frequently ordered by the physician when it is desirable to unite great nourishment with easy digestion, the amount of gluten they contain giving them this valuable quality.

Lobsters are popularly considered to be the least harmful next to oysters, and the flesh of a fresh crab is both delicate and delicious.

Shrimps, prawns, and crayfish, should properly rank as "relishes"; they are extremely useful in savoury dishes, either with or without other fish.

Cockles are deservedly esteemed by the rich, and they have often staved off the pressure of starvation from the poor of our coasts.

The limpet is a great favourite with the Irish, while the periwinkle is the poor man's luxury, and the clam enjoys high favour in the United States.

PART I.

CHOOSING AND BUYING FISH.

Before coming to this important part of our subject, we would like to offer a suggestion (in all courtesy, be it understood) to our friends the fishmongers.

Why do they, we would ask, invariably establish themselves on the sunny side of the road? Surely if any branch of trade requires coolness and shade it is the fish trade, yet how rare an exception to find one so situated. Then we would respectfully draw their attention to their way of handling the fish. Often it receives most unmerciful treatment, being knocked about on the marble slab with a force quite unnecessary. All fish suffer more or less, but delicate fish, such as soles, suffer in this way just as a ripe peach or pear does if subjected to the same treatment. The same difference can be detected in the bruised part of fish as in a bruised peach.

Also a too liberal pouring-on of water is injurious. No doubt the bright and well-washed fish, surrounded with lumps of ice, look far more tempting than the boat-load all smeared with blood, yet the fish would be much better if they did not see fresh water until they are to be dressed at home. In this matter, however, the fishmonger is to a large extent ruled by popular opinion, and if the latter forbids the purchase of fish in their more natural condition, he is perhaps justified in endeavouring to suit the fancy of his customers.

In choosing fish care should be taken not to judge too much by first appearances, although, fortunately, fish, if not fresh, soon tells its tale.

If the eyes are dull, or the skin and the scales rub off easily, *avoid that fish*. If the skin is bright, the flesh firm to the touch when pressed between the thumb and finger, you may rely upon its being fresh; stale fish, or that which has been kept long in ice, is always flabby.

One safe general direction for choosing fish may be given in few words, viz., *choose the plump ones*.

A short fish, thick about the shoulders, is much to be preferred to a long thin one. Thick soles, or thick turbots, are far preferable to thin ones. The same with codfish.

Lobsters and crabs should be chosen by weight, and those of medium size are best in flavour.

There are one or two kinds of fish which are positively improved by being kept a day or two, notably skate and red mullet.

Mackerel, on the contrary, is a fish than which none spoils more rapidly.

The sole holds a first position among flat fish, and is deservedly esteemed, as its flesh is firm and delicate and very easily digested, hence its great popularity with the sick. It has also the advantage of being obtainable all the year round in good condition. The skin of the back is sometimes dark, sometimes white, varying with the nature of the ground on which the fish feeds. Soles vary in size from quite little slips, called "tongues," to large fish weighing eight or nine pounds per pair. Those in roe are rather insipid in flavour, and are best for filleting. They vary in price, but are never a *cheap* fish.

Halibut is an excellent substitute for turbot, which it rather resembles in flavour, and is a comparatively cheap fish. It is abundant in spring and summertime, and always a favourite with Jewish people. Being a very large fish, it is rarely sold entire. The choice bits are the flackers over the fins and the pickings about the head.

A fillet or "steak" is the most profitable portion for general eating.

Cod is at its best about Christmas time. From the end of January to March it is less good and not abundant; in May again it is generally very fine. The best are those which are plump and round at the tail, the sides having a slightly ribbed appearance, with yellow spots on a clear skin.

Large cod are not generally cooked whole, being so much thicker at the head than at the tail. The head and shoulders, usually sold apart, form a handsome dish.

It is a very nourishing fish, valuable in many ways, and if its "adaptabilities" were more understood it would be more generally appreciated.

The salmon has been called the "king of fresh-water fish," yet, as before remarked, it does not belong to this category.

The river is its birthplace, it is true, but the sea is its pasture ground, where it returns periodically to renew its strength. It inhabits fresh and salt water alternately, spending its summer in the river and its winter in the sea. Just as the swallow returns again to the same roof which sheltered it, so the salmon returns again to the same river. This fact has been taken advantage of to naturalise salmon in rivers where formerly there were no signs of them. No stranger salmon cruising along the coast will mistake another river's mouth for the mouth of its own river.

The flesh is rich and delicious in flavour, and to be eaten in perfection it should be dressed as soon as caught; there will then be found between the flakes a creamy-white substance called "curd," which is highly esteemed by the epicure. Nevertheless, it is then highly indigestible; to be perfectly wholesome eating the salmon should be kept twenty-four hours, then the curd solidifies, and though perhaps less delicate in flavour, it is richer and far less likely to disagree.

In season from February to August; it is at its cheapest in July and August.

Salmon trout, though resembling salmon in flavour and appearance, are really not at all the same species. They rarely exceed two to three pounds in weight—generally they are but three-quarters of a pound. They are justly regarded as a great delicacy, and are at their best in spring and early summer. The flesh is sometimes white, sometimes red; the latter is the most prized.

When choosing salmon trout examine the inside of the throat through the gills. If this is very red the flesh will prove to be red, though not so red as salmon.

There are two or three kinds of trout: common, sea, and white trout. Sea trout reaches a good size, white trout never does. River trout are most delicious and highly esteemed; the most delicate in flavour are those which weigh from three-quarters to one pound.

Trout, which is in season from May to September, is in perfection in June.

Carp and tench are pond rather than river fish, and both have a great fondness for burying themselves in mud, and owing to this the flesh has often a slight muddy taste; for this reason the fish should lie in strong salt and water for a few hours, then be well cleansed in clear spring water.

Both are at their best in the winter months. The tench, though a smaller fish, is richer and more delicate than the carp. They are useful fish to families residing in the country.

Although the pike attains to a considerable size in England, it is small in comparison with its brethren found in Russian and Lapland waters. Indeed it more truly deserves to be called a Russian fish, so much more abundant and popular is it there. In colour the skin is a pale olive-grey, with several yellowish spots on the sides, and the mouth is furnished with a prodigious number of teeth, which has earned for it the name of "fresh-water shark."

It was at one time a very popular article of food, and is still considered a good fish for the table. In some countries the fish is salted and dried, and the roe made into caviare.

The perch, which is one of the commonest of our fresh-water fish, is also one of the best. It is met with in almost all lakes and rivers in temperate regions. When full-grown it is a large fish, although one weighing a pound is thought a good size, and one of three pounds very large. The flesh is white, firm, of a good flavour, and easily digested.

Perch are so tenacious of life, they may be carried fifty miles and yet survive the journey.

Best used as soon as caught, they are also better for being crimped as soon as they leave the water. Their season is from June to February.

Perhaps the most commonly used fish is the herring. Shoals of herring visit the British Islands from the end of May till October, and even occasionally during the winter months. In the beginning of the season the fish is rather oily, and often found to be indigestible on that account, but after the first few weeks this disappears, and then it becomes both digestible and nourishing.

In choosing herrings take care that they feel firm, and have bright eyes and scales.

Sprats closely resemble herrings in appearance and flavour, only they are but a third of the size of the latter. They are very abundant on the North British coasts, and in Edinburgh and Glasgow are sold by measure. Their best season is the winter time, and their freshness may be judged by their silvery appearance—or otherwise.

The highly esteemed smelt is a most delicate fish. When fresh it possesses an odour like a freshly-cut cucumber, but this perfume passes away twelve hours after it has been caught.

The Dutch fisheries furnish very fine smelts, and the baskets full of bright silvery little bodies look very tempting in the wholesale market. These are never what may be called cheap fish. In season from November to May. Smelts which have been split and dried are called sparlings.

Another fish which is cheap and plentiful in the winter months is the haddock. They seldom weigh more than from three to four pounds, and the largest are considered the best. They should be gutted as soon as possible, and hung up to dry with salt inside them. Scotch haddock have the highest reputation.

Among lesser known fish are the gurnet, dory, and ling. All of them are excellent eating. The dory resembles the turbot in flavour, and the gurnet has firm white flesh, of agreeable taste. In the early spring months ling is captured in large quantities off the Orkney and Shetland Isles.

Skate and plaice are both less thought of in England than they deserve to be; in France they are better appreciated. Skate improves by being hung up for a day before using. Young skate are called "maids," and their flesh is tender and delicate.

Plaice is in good condition when the body is thick and firm, the eyes bright, and the pale side tinged with pink.

Hake, or "white salmon," is a west-country fish, common in Devonshire. In season in the autumn months.

Eels and lampreys, very rich, and not over wholesome, are mostly food for the epicure. They are useful in cookery where a succulent dish is required. The lamprey is but little met with in the present day.

PART II.

THE COOKING OF FISH.

The recipes given in this part have been gleaned from reliable sources. Many of them are from French cooks, and are strictly in accordance with the methods in use in the best "cuisines," where the cooking of fish receives great care and attention.

For greater convenience in reference the recipes for preparing the different kinds of fish are all classed under the name of each kind, and the names given in alphabetical order.

Perhaps the only ways of properly cooking fish are baking and broiling, yet these are precisely the ways least practised—out of France. Boiling and frying have hitherto held too great a monopoly in our methods. In the following pages, while giving the latter modes their due share of attention, we beg to call for special notice to be given to the examples for *broiling*, &c., as they may be relied upon to bring about a satisfactory result if carefully followed.

To begin with a few general directions:

In broiling a perfectly clear fire is *absolutely indispensable*; more so in the case of fish than when intending to cook steak or chops. A shovel-full of good cinders, slightly wetted, and given sufficient time to become red-hot, will generally ensure a good surface heat, but a charcoal "braisière" is *par-excellence* the fire for this purpose, and no French housewife considers her kitchen complete without this little contrivance. A little charcoal sprinkled over some hot coals is not a bad substitute for it.

A special gridiron should be kept for fish only. After using, let it be thoroughly washed and dried, and before using again rub the bars over with a little oil; fish is more easily marked, and apt to stick sooner than meat.

If the gridiron is not a double one, use a pair of sugar-tongs with which to turn the fish over; beware of sticking a fork into it. There can be no doubt that grilling brings out a flavour which nothing else will.

What can surpass a fresh mackerel, grilled after being split open and boned?

An important point to bear in mind in this method of cookery is, to *keep in the flavour*. A slice of grilled salmon will taste far nicer if the slice has been wrapped in buttered paper; but cooking anything in paper requires the greatest care, as should there be the least flare the paper will catch fire,—what is required is a fierce heat.

When baking fish *en papillot*, that is wrapped in buttered paper, the chief thing to bear in mind is not to spare the butter. This, one of the most delicate and delicious ways of cooking fish, is apt to be entirely spoilt, because only a little dab of butter is allowed. When fish has been cooked in paper it should be sent to table just as it is, paper and all. Always use plain white note paper, never printed.

In boiling fish a very common fault is omitting to put sufficient salt into the water. In the case of large fish, salt should be added in the proportion of half a pound to a gallon of water; for smaller fish, a proportion of a quarter-pound to the gallon is sufficient.

It is now generally thought best to place fish in nearly boiling water, then allow it to come gently to the boiling point again, this keeps in the flavour on the same principle as the boiling of meat. The time allowed depends entirely on the size of the fish, but when the flesh shows signs of being just able to be separated from the bone, it is amply done.

Experience is the only safe guide.

To preserve the *whiteness* of white fish, it is wise to rub them over with lemon-juice before boiling.

One method of boiling fish, when it is intended for eating cold, which is much approved of on the Continent, is to do it in "court-bouillon," and if fresh-water fish be cooked this way it is relieved of much of its insipidity.

One part of vinegar, one part of red wine, to four parts of water, for the "bouillon." To two quarts of the liquor put an ounce of salt, half an ounce of pepper, a bunch of savoury herbs, a sliced onion and a carrot. Sometimes a small piece of salt bacon is also added. Let these all boil together for some time, then strain the liquor and keep in a stone jar. It will keep a long time if occasionally re-boiled.

The fish should be well covered with the liquid when laid in the fish- kettle, and allowed to boil gradually.

To fry fish successfully it should be literally *boiled* in fat. This cannot be done over a slow or smoky fire, neither can it be done unless an abundance of fat be allowed. It is not an extravagant method, even if the pan be a large one, and it takes two or three pounds to fill it. If carefully poured into a basin containing boiling water after the fish has been cooked, the loose breadcrumbs and other particles will fall to the bottom, and the fat form a clear white crust. When due care is exercised there is no reason why the same fat should not be used fifty times over.

Let it be quite boiling when the fish is put in. This may be known by its perfect stillness and the faint blue vapour which will rise from it. When the fish has been washed and carefully dried, flour it before dipping into beaten egg, and use brown raspings in preference to breadcrumbs.

Lay a small piece of blotting-paper at the bottom of the dish to absorb all grease.

Various recipes for *baking* fish are given in the following pages. Perhaps one of the nicest ways of doing fish in the oven is *au gratin*. Briefly described, this consists of a layer of mixed herbs and breadcrumbs laid first at the bottom of a well-buttered dish, the fish laid on this, then the same ingredients with seasoning and more butter over it. Very often a glass of wine or vinegar is added.

Anything cooked *au gratin* must always come to table in the dish in which it was cooked, hence the gratin-dish, sometimes of silver, sometimes of polished tin or fire-proof china, is another kitchen requisite almost indispensable.

When intending to use salted fish for any dish it should always be allowed to lie in water at least twenty-four hours previously, and the water should be changed frequently; then drain and dry thoroughly.

PART III.

TESTED RECIPES.

Anchovies are the only fish which come under this letter. They are usually bought in pickle from grocers and oilmen, and ought to soak in cold water before they are used. The small, plump ones are the best—the pickle is red, the scales of the fish white. If cut into fillets and added to sliced cucumber, hard-boiled egg, also sliced, minced parsley and herbs, and dressed with the usual salad dressing, they form an acceptable variety in the salad series.

Anchovies, Essence of (home-made), is made by beating to a paste half-a-pound of anchovies, bones also, then adding a pint of raisin wine to the paste and boiling both together until it is dissolved. For seasoning add a very small quantity of cayenne pepper, two or three Jamaica peppercorns and three or four shallots. Home-made essence is greatly superior in flavour to that which can be bought.

Anchovy Butter is prepared by pounding to a paste half-a-pound of anchovies with half that weight of butter. A pinch of cayenne is an improvement. This butter is especially useful for flavouring sauces for meat and fish, and if kept in very small pots, closely covered, it will remain good for some time. *Anchovy Paste*, so much liked for sandwiches, is made in the same way.

Anchovy Sauce.—Two ounces of butter melted, two tablespoonfuls of flour mixed smoothly with it, a tumblerful of boiling water. When this has boiled stir in gradually three teaspoonfuls of the essence of anchovies, and add the juice of half a lemon; let all boil once more, then pour into a tureen.

Barbel.—This is but a poor fish, being woolly and rather flavourless. It may be made palatable by cutting in pieces, then steeping in a marinade of oil, pepper and salt, for half an hour, after which broil the pieces over the fire, and serve with *maître d'hôtel* butter.

Bloaters.—The smoked bloaters should be scalded with boiling water, then dried. The bones can often be drawn off after this, before cooking. They may either be broiled over the fire for a moment, or cooked in the oven with a morsel of butter.

Before broiling fresh bloaters split them open down the middle, remove the backbone and cleanse them. Sprinkle with pepper and salt, and drop a morsel of butter on each before bringing to table.

Bream is a handsome, although not a delicate fish. It must be thoroughly cleansed and washed out with vinegar. Split it open and remove the bone, but do not scale it. It is best broiled, but is excellent if stuffed with a little forcemeat, then baked in the oven for twenty minutes. Melted butter, caper sauce, or anchovy sauce, must accompany it to table.

Brill.—This fish has an excellent reputation, resembling turbot so nearly; it may be cooked in almost every way recommended for the latter. Thick brill are the best, and a yellowish hue in the flesh denotes its freshness. Lay it in salted water for a few minutes, then dry it and rub with the juice of a lemon. When boiling brill allow plenty of salt in the water, and half a teacupful of lemon juice. Let it simmer gently after reaching boiling point till just tender through. Lay on a clean serviette, the white side uppermost, garnish with cut lemon and parsley, also a sprinkling of lobster coral.

Carp, Baked.—After washing and scaling, remove the inside of the carp, squeeze over it the juice of one or two lemons and let it lie thus for an hour. Next place it in a baking tin, sprinkle some minced parsley and shallots over it, also pepper and salt, then pour a little oiled butter over all. Cover with white paper and bake for upwards of forty minutes—gently. Make a little thick melted butter, enrich it further with a spoonful of cream, stir in the juice of half a lemon, and more salt and pepper—cayenne if liked. Lift the carp on to a dish, pour this sauce over it, garnish with chopped gherkins and lobster coral.

Carp, Fried.—Cut the fish into fillets after having thoroughly cleansed it. Roll each fillet in flour seasoned with salt and cayenne. Fry in a depth of boiling fat, serve with anchovy sauce.

Carp, Grilled.—Only very small carp can be cooked this way, and they should be wrapped in buttered papers, after having been washed and emptied. Serve with a piquant sauce of minced herbs, lemon-juice and butter.

Carp, Stewed.—Carp are excellent treated this way if rather large. After washing in vinegar and water, cut the fish into fair-sized pieces, roll each piece in seasoned flour, then lay in a covered stewpan, and pour a tumblerful of white wine over them. Allow nearly an hour for the cooking, then when done remove the pieces of fish carefully on to a dish, stir in a tablespoonful of grated horseradish, a little cream, and the beaten yolk of an egg into the sauce, and pour it over the carp.

If boiled in "court-bouillon," carp is equally good for eating cold.

Caveach Fish.—Clean some large fish, such as cod or salmon, then cut them into slices. Rub each slice with salt, pepper and spice, and fry in boiling fat till lightly browned. Let them drain and get quite cold, then lay in deep jars. Boil some vinegar with a few shallots, peppercorns, a bay leaf and blade of mace; when this is cold fill the jars nearly full with this, pour a little salad oil on the top and cover closely. They will keep for months, and when required the slices are lifted out, placed in the centre of a dish with dressed salad round them.

Clams.—Clams, which are a species of cockle, were declared by the great Soyer to be superior to the oyster in flavour. They are very nice if fried, after dipping into beaten egg and breadcrumbs. In America they are stewed. Put into a stewpan with a little water, they are boiled for a few minutes, then seasoned with pepper and salt.

Cockles.—Cockles should be roasted on a tin laid on the top of a stove; they are eaten whilst hot with bread and butter. They require to be well washed, and the shells scrubbed with a brush.

Cod, Baked.—Take a piece weighing about three pounds out of the middle of a large fish. Make a simple forcemeat of breadcrumbs, minced parsley, thyme, seasoning, and the yolk of an egg; put this inside the fish and sew it up. Place in a baking-dish, and surround with a carrot sliced, and also a turnip and small onion. Pour a spoonful of vinegar over, and place two or three lumps of butter on the top; bake for twenty minutes. Remove the vegetables, but serve the liquor with the fish instead of sauce.

Cod, Fried à la Maître d'Hôtel.—Take two or three slices of cod about an inch and a half in thickness, let them lie in salt water for half an hour, then drain and dry them. Cover with seasoned flour, and fry in a quantity of boiling fat for a few minutes. Pile in pyramid form on a hot dish, pouring the following sauce round them: two tablespoonsful of fresh green parsley chopped small, two ounces of butter, half an ounce of flour, a little salt, pepper, and a spoonful of vinegar; add a little water if it thickens too much. Mix the ingredients well, let them boil up once, then serve.

Cod, à la Crème.—The remains of boiled cod will do excellently well for this, or if fresh fish is used it must be first boiled till tender, then broken into flakes, all skin and bone removed. Into a saucepan put a pint of milk with a teaspoonful of salt and the rind of a lemon. Let this boil once, then pour off into a basin. In the saucepan melt an ounce of butter and stir in smoothly an ounce of flour, add a pinch of cayenne pepper, then the milk, and boil all together until thick. Put in the flakes of cod to heat through, then pour all on to a hot dish, garnish with tufts of parsley, and pass round strips of toasted bread to eat with it.

Cod, Curried.—Take the remains of cold boiled cod broken into
flakes, fry them a moment in butter. Lay them aside on a hot plate and prepare the curry. For this put an ounce of butter into a saucepan and slice into it two shallots and one small apple. When these have frizzled brown stir in a tablespoonful of flour, half a teaspoonful of curry powder, the same of salt, and a pinch of cayenne pepper, and lastly a teacupful of stock. Let this boil a few minutes, then put in the cod to warm up, and serve quickly. A wall of boiled rice round the edge of the dish is an improvement.

Cod, Salted, with Parsnips.—Take a couple of pounds of salted
cod, let it soak for twenty-four hours, then drain, and pouring fresh cold water over it let it heat through gradually. It should simmer until tender, but must not boil, or it will become hard. Drain again, lay on a hot dish, garnish with boiled parsnips cut into lengths, and cover all with egg sauce, made as follows: half a pint of milk thickened with flour, a small bit of butter, salt, pepper, the juice of a lemon, and two hard-boiled eggs chopped small and stirred in. Garnish the dish with parsley.

Cod, Salted, en Mousse.—Soak and cook the cod as in the
previous recipe, then drain and break into flakes. Frizzle a slice of a Spanish onion in a small quantity of butter, but do not brown it. Scald the soft part of a slice of white bread, break it with a fork, then add to the onion, and at the same time add gradually a cupful of new milk. Continue to beat until all is quite smooth, sprinkle with salt and pepper, then add the flakes of cod, still continuing to beat. If becoming too stiff add more milk. When all is light and like a froth, pour on to a dish and dot small bits of fried or toasted crusts about the surface.

Cod, Head and Shoulders Boiled.—A portion or the whole
of a large fish, when intended for boiling, should be previously crimped, when it should receive some deep cuts as far as the bone on both sides. Afterwards it should lie in vinegar and water for half an hour. It should be plunged at once into boiling water, then allowed to simmer till just tender.

Drain, and serve on a white d'oyley, garnished with lemon and parsley. Crimping renders the flesh firmer, and makes it easier both to cook and to serve.

Crab.—The crabs which have a rough shell and claws are the best. When choosing one shake it well; if it rattle it is sure to prove watery. The shell should be of a bright red, and the eyes look clear. In picking out the meat from the shell and claws leave out the part near the head, which is not fit to be eaten.

Crab, Hot Buttered.—Pick the meat from the shell of a crab, mix with half its quantity of breadcrumbs, a little pepper, salt, grated nutmeg, a spoonful of salad oil and the same of vinegar. Clean the empty shell, then refill it with this mixture, sprinkle more crumbs over the top, then a nob of butter, and bake for nearly ten minutes. To eat with hot dry toast.

Crab, Salad.—Pick the meat from the shell into flakes, make a pile in the centre of a dish, leaving the claws on the top; surround with shred lettuce and watercress, and pour a simple salad dressing over all.

Crab Soup, or Potage Bisque.—This is most delicious and delicate. Choose a nice heavy crab, pick out the meat from the claws into shreds. The soft meat from the inside of the body is pounded in a mortar with half its quantity of boiled rice; this is thinned a little with some clear stock, then passed through a colander. Put this into a stewpan with sufficient stock to make the required quantity (veal stock is preferable), add a cupful of thickened cream, salt to taste, and a little cayenne pepper, let it boil once only, then take from the fire and add the shredded meat from the claws. A little lobster butter stirred in will make it a richer colour.

Make potage from lobster or crayfish in exactly the same manner. The result will be almost as satisfactory.

Crayfish.—Crayfish resemble lobsters in flavour, but they are smaller, and the flesh is more delicate. Those which are red under the claws are the best. Wash them well, and boil in salt water for ten minutes, after which they will become a bright red. Drain well, then pile in pyramid form, and garnish with parsley.

A pretty dish may be made from them by preparing a clear savoury jelly, and arranging the crayfish in a fancy mould—minus the tails—filling in all spaces with the jelly.

Crayfish, as a Breakfast Relish.—Remove the tails from a pint of crayfish, put the bodies to simmer gently in a saucepan with an ounce of butter, a teacupful of water, a spoonful of vinegar, grate of nutmeg, and a little salt and pepper. Simmer for ten minutes, thicken with flour, and pour over a slice of toast.

Crayfish may also be potted like shrimps.

Dabs.—These insignificant little fish are caught in the mouths of rivers near the sea. They are nice if fried, but more tasty if wrapped in buttered paper and baked for fifteen minutes. Send to table with sliced lemon.

Dace.—This fish scarcely repays the trouble of cooking, and is usually only enjoyed by the angler who has caught it. It may be either fried or boiled. A little sharp sauce with lemon juice and mustard are almost necessary accompaniments.

Dory.—Although by no means a handsome fish, yet the dory has a flavour which makes it excellent eating. It is best boiled, or rather *simmered*, after it has boiled once, twenty minutes for a fair-sized fish. Serve on a napkin, garnished with parsley. Anchovy, shrimp, or caper sauce, are all suitable for serving with boiled dory.

Eels, en Matelote.—Skin and clean about two pounds of eels, divide into pieces of two inches long, let them lie in salt water while some onions are being fried in butter. When the onions have browned, stir in flour to absorb all the butter, then a cupful of stock and the same of red wine, a few mushrooms, pepper and salt, and a pinch of herbs. Stew the eels in this gravy until thoroughly tender, about forty minutes. Serve altogether.

Eels, Boiled, for Invalids.—When the skin has been drawn off the eel, and it has lain in salt water to cleanse it, it should be placed before a clear fire for ten minutes to draw out the oil. Wash again in warm water, and set to boil in a saucepan with a bunch of parsley and spoonful of salt. When tender take it out, divide into lengths, thicken a small quantity of the broth, add cream and chopped parsley, and pour over the eel.

Findon, or "Finnan," Haddocks.—The Findon haddock, so highly esteemed for its delicate flavour, may be distinguished by its odour and creamy yellow colour. The skin should be stripped off, and the fish broiled quickly over a clear fire. Rub butter over it before bringing to table.

Flounders.—Flounders may be boiled, baked, fried, or stewed. As they are apt to have a slight muddy flavour, they should lie in salt water for a while. Perhaps the nicest way of cooking them is to dip them into beaten egg, cover with raspings, and boil them in fat.

Flounders may also be done *au gratin*, by laying the fish (neatly trimmed) on a bed of chopped shallots and parsley, breadcrumbs and butter, covering them with the same, then adding a glass of white wine, and baking for twenty minutes. Allow at least one for each person.

Gurnet.—The head of the gurnet is large in comparison with the rest of the body. It is apt to be a dirty fish, and needs very thorough cleansing. The gills should be cut off. Perhaps the best way of cooking it is to remove the head and the inside, stuff it with a forcemeat, sew the body up and lay it in a deep tin, covering with a slice or two of salt fat. Bake for half an hour, then remove on to a hot dish, and pour *maître d'hôtel* butter over it.

Haddock, Broiled.—Draw and clean the haddock very thoroughly, wiping it perfectly dry. Dredge with flour, then pour a little salad oil over it. Lay on the gridiron and broil quickly. When brown and crisp it is done. Serve with anchovy sauce.

Haddock, Baked.—Empty and wash the fish, scaling it carefully; let it lie in vinegar for fifteen minutes, then dry it, dredge with flour, cover with beaten egg, then with breadcrumbs, and lay in a greased baking-dish. Pour melted butter over it, and bake about twenty minutes. The gravy which comes from the fish may be seasoned and sent to table with it. Garnish with cut lemons.

Haddock, Curried.—Choose small haddocks for this purpose. Split them open, remove bones and the head, divide into convenient-sized pieces. Dip each piece into seasoned flour and fry till crisp and brown. Prepare a curry sauce by frizzling a small onion and an apple in butter, thickening with flour, adding seasoning and a little curry powder and clear stock to make the requisite quantity. Put the fish into this sauce to heat through, then pile in the centre of a dish and pour the sauce over. Garnish with rice.

Halibut.—Being very large fish, perhaps the most satisfactory way of dealing with halibut is to cut them into steaks, viz., slices across the fish of any thickness desired. They may be either broiled or fried. When broiling, sprinkle them with seasoning, and let them lie in salad oil for a few minutes, then drain and broil quickly over a bright fire. Lay on a hot dish, squeeze lemon juice over, and sprinkle with chopped parsley.

For frying, the steaks may be either dredged with flour, or dipped in egg and breadcrumbs, then fried in a shallow depth of fat till lightly brown. Drain on blotting paper, and send shrimp or anchovy sauce to table with them.

Boiling is the least satisfactory way of cooking halibut, but if it be chosen, have the fish in one thick piece. Put into boiling water, and simmer gently until the fish shows signs of parting from the bone.

Halibut Pie.—Take a piece of the middle of the fish, remove all skin, and cut into pieces an inch square. Roll each piece in a mixture of salt, pepper, and breadcrumbs, place in a pie-dish with lumps of butter at the top. Pour a glass of white wine over. Cover with a "short" crust, and when this has baked until well brown, the fish also will be done.

Herrings, Boiled.—Few fish are more delicious than fresh herrings boiled. Wash, scale, and empty them very particularly. Souse them with vinegar, then drop into boiling salted water, simmer for about ten minutes, and lift them out the moment they are done. Drain them, arrange nicely on a clean napkin, garnish with parsley and horseradish, and serve parsley sauce with them.

Herrings, Broiled.—Let them lie in salt overnight, wash them, empty, and split them open. Dry thoroughly, and dredge a little flour over them. Lay on an oiled gridiron, broil on both sides. Lay each one separately on a hot plate, and place a morsel of butter on the top. Then pour the following sauce over them: a tablespoonful of chopped parsley, the same of minced herbs, and a "suspicion" of onion, same of butter, a teaspoonful of salt and pepper mixed, a wineglassful of vinegar; boil altogether for a moment.

Herrings, Pickled (to eat cold).—Scale and clean the herrings carefully, split them open and take out the backbone. Sprinkle with salt and pepper after laying in a deep dish. Cover with vinegar and water. Bake till tender through.

Herrings, Pickled (French mode).—Scale and clean the herrings, empty without splitting them. Cut off the heads, and put the fish into an earthern jar, strew salt liberally over them; let them lie twenty-four hours. Drain them and place them in an enamelled saucepan with a dozen peppercorns, a bay-leaf or two, and an onion with a clove. Cover with cold vinegar. Let them come to boiling point, and boil two minutes only. Stand aside until quite cold, when they may be placed in a covered jar. They will keep good for some time.

Lampreys, Stewed.—Rub the lamprey well with salt, and wash it in water (warm) to get rid of the slime. Cut off the head, tail, and gills, empty it, then cut into pieces three inches long. Slice three or four onions into the bottom of a stewpan, dip each piece of lamprey into flour, and lay over the onions. Add next a dozen mushrooms, a tablespoonful of chopped parsley, grated lemon-rind and a little juice, pepper, and salt. A glassful of red wine and sufficient stock to cover the whole, replace the lid, and stew gently for two hours. Serve altogether.

Ling, Baked.—Cleanse and empty the fish, cut it into thick slices, removing the head and tail. Dredge the slices with flour, and sprinkle with salt and pepper. Lay them in a baking-dish, and pour some melted butter over them. Bake for twenty minutes, place the slices of fish on a hot dish, then add a cupful of cream and a small tinful of button mushrooms to the butter, make thoroughly hot and pour over the fish just before bringing to table.

Or, the slices of ling may be dipped into beaten egg, covered with raspings, and fried in hot fat, a *sauce rémoulade* being brought to table with them.

Lobster, à la Crème.—Pick the meat from a fresh lobster without breaking the shell; cut it into dice. Put into an enamelled saucepan with a mixed teaspoonful of salt, pepper, and nutmeg, a glassful of white wine, a tablespoonful of vinegar, and an ounce of butter rolled in flour. Simmer gently for ten minutes, stirring all the time. Then stir in two tablespoonfuls of thickened cream. Pour the mixture into the shell of the lobster, cover the top with breadcrumbs, brown quickly in the oven, then set the shell on a folded napkin, and garnish with parsley.

Lobster Cutlets.—A large lobster is required for these. Boil for five minutes, then crack the shell and take out the meat as whole as possible. Cut this across in slices a quarter of an inch in thickness. Dip each slice into beaten egg and breadcrumbs, sprinkle with salt and pepper, and fry in fat for about five minutes. Make a small mound of whipped potato for the centre of a dish, arrange the cutlets round this, and send oyster sauce to table with them.

Lobster Patties.—Boil a lobster for fifteen minutes. Crack it open and pick the meat out into flakes. Put the flakes into an enamelled saucepan with an ounce of butter, a tablespoonful of cream, same of white stock, and a teaspoonful of essence of anchovies, a little seasoning also, and a few dry breadcrumbs. Boil up for a moment. Line some patty-pans with good puff paste not rolled too thinly, place a morsel of crumb of bread in the middle before putting on the top crust; bake the patties a bright brown, lift off the top crust, take out the bread, fill with the hot mixture, and replace the cover.

Serve very hot.

Lobster Salad.—For this the lobster is required very sweet and fresh; it should have been boiled about twenty minutes and then have become quite cold. Crack the shell and remove the meat as whole as possible, saving the coral for garnishing. Divide the meat into small neat pieces, seasoning each with salt, pepper, and vinegar. Take two lettuces with firm, white hearts, wipe them clean with a cloth. They must be crisp and perfectly dry. Place first a layer of shred lettuce at the bottom of a bowl, then a layer of seasoned lobster; alternate till the stock is exhausted. Pour the following dressing over all at the last moment, and sprinkle the coral over the surface. A fanciful outer edge may be made of sliced eggs and beetroot, or nasturtium flowers, radishes set in parsley, &c.

Dressing.—The yolks of two eggs beaten until thick, a saltspoonful of salt, half of pepper, same of made mustard. Beat in slowly half a pint of oil and two spoonsful of vinegar.

Lobster Butter, and Sauce.—The spawn and coral of a freshly-boiled hen lobster, pounded together in a mortar with twice their quantity of fresh butter and a spice of cayenne pepper, makes lobster butter. It should be of a bright red colour. Keep in small pots well covered, and in a cool place.

For the sauce, make some good plain melted butter, pick out a few flakes of the white meat of a lobster, then stir in a spoonful of the lobster butter. Do not boil it after this, or the colour will be spoilt. The juice of a lemon may be added if liked.

Mackerel, Broiled.—For a perfectly fresh, small, plump mackerel, this is *the* mode of cooking *par excellence*.

Cleanse the fish thoroughly, and dry them first with a cloth, then by hanging up in the open air. Split them open flat and carefully remove the backbone. Smear them with salad oil, sprinkle them with salt and pepper, wrap each one in a fold of buttered note-paper, and lay on the gridiron. Broil carefully over a clear *red* fire for twenty minutes, turning occasionally. They may be broiled without the paper, in which case fifteen minutes will be more than long enough, but will taste less delicate and be less easily digested. Lay on a hot dish, cover closely, and serve with or without *maître d'hôtel* butter.

Mackerel, Baked.—Large mackerel are preferable for this mode. After cleaning and taking out the roes, fill with the following forcemeat:—
Three ounces of breadcrumbs, an ounce of finely-shred beef suet, the same of

chopped parsley, a pinch of savoury herbs, minced chives, and pepper and salt. Bind the mixture with a beaten egg. When the fish has been filled, sew the sides together with strong thread, lay it on a baking dish, dredge a little flour over it, and pour over either some melted butter or clarified fat. Bake twenty minutes. Serve with the same butter to the which some chopped parsley has been added, or with a *sauce piquante.*

Mackerel, Boiled.—Wash and empty them without splitting them more than can be helped. Lay them in *hot* water with plenty of salt. Let the water come to a boil, then draw aside and simmer them till the skin shows signs of breaking. Drain, and serve on a clean serviette. Garnish with parsley. Serve either parsley or fennel sauce with them.

Mullet, Red.—These fish are much the best if cooked in buttered paper. They may be roast, baked, or boiled—all ways are excellent if the precaution of wrapping up be observed. A liberal share of butter should be enclosed with them. The gills and fins only are removed; the inside remains untouched, as the liver is much esteemed. Cook them about twenty-five minutes, take out of the papers, and serve with plenty of sauce in a tureen. Add the liquor which has oozed from the fish to some plain melted butter, with a spoonful of anchovy sauce, a squeeze of lemon juice, and a glassful of some good red wine.

Mullet, Red (Broiled *à la maître d'hôtel*).—Clean the mullet and empty them, score them across in several places, lay them to soak in a marinade of salad oil and minced sweet herbs—garlic also if the taste is liked. Let them lie in this for half an hour. Drain them, sprinkle with salt and pepper, lay on a gridiron, and broil over a clear fire, turning on both sides.

Mullet, Grey.—The grey mullet is but seldom offered for sale. It is generally thought much inferior to the red, and is only seasonable during the heat of summer. It may be cooked in any of the ways given for mackerel or for red mullet.

Oysters.—Oysters are never so excellent or so easy of digestion as when they are eaten straight out of the newly-opened shell. If carefully opened, and none of the juice be spilt, they will need no seasoning; but if it be preferred, salt and pepper may be sprinkled over them, also a squeeze of lemon juice. Brown bread and butter is the usual accompaniment to them.

Oysters, Browned in their own gravy.—This is a very dainty dish. Take a dozen or more large oysters, open them carefully, and pour the juice from each one into a cup. Take off the beards, dip each oyster into beaten egg thickened with flour. Brown them in a little butter, lift them out, add the gravy from the cup to the butter, thicken with flour, and season with pepper and salt. Let it simmer for two or three minutes, then stir in the browned oysters; let them heat through again, then pour over a slice of toast.

Oysters, au Gratin.—Butter a bright tin or silver gratin-dish. Stir into a few ounces of breadcrumbs a spoonful of chopped parsley and sweet herbs with seasoning. Sprinkle these thickly over the butter, and moisten with white wine. Then split open two dozen large oysters, take off the beards, and lay each oyster on the bed in the dish, pouring the juice over as well. Cover them with a few more crumbs, place three or four nobs of butter on the top, and bake in a moderate oven for ten minutes. Bring to table in the dish.

Perch.—The best way of dressing perch is in *water souchy.* Remember always to clean the perch first with a little warm water to take off the slime, then lay them in cold salt water for an hour or so. Pick out the smallest of the fish for the *souchy*, empty them, cut into pieces, boil them slowly with some parsley-root, peppercorns, and salt. Strain the broth (for the ingredients should boil until a strong broth is obtained) through a muslin. The large perch should be crimped, after being cleaned, then placed in the broth and simmered until just tender. Drain them, serve in a deep dish with a ladleful of the broth poured over them, and garnished with green parsley. A little fresh parsley, chopped, may be introduced into the broth if liked.

Perch may also be laid in a marinade (after being cleansed) then broiled over the fire. It is well if, after lifting them out of the marinade, they are liberally besprinkled with seasoned breadcrumbs and herbs. Broil till lightly browned, lay on a hot dish, a nob of butter on each, and garnish. Serve a little sharp sauce with them.

If economy is not to be studied, they are very nice if stewed in wine—sherry, or equal parts of sherry and clear stock. Lay the perch in a deep dish, and just cover them with the above. Slice an onion very thinly, lay over them with a few sprigs of parsley, thyme, a bay-leaf, and some peppercorns, sprinkle liberally with salt, and let them simmer gently for about twenty minutes. Make a sauce from the liquor by thickening it with butter rolled in flour, and serve poured over the fish.

Pike, Baked.—Pike must be scaled after washing them. To scale it easily, first pour boiling water over the fish, then plunge immediately into cold water, and scrape briskly with the back of a knife. Wipe the fish dry, then empty it, and fill the cavity with a nicely seasoned forcemeat, sew up the sides, and lay in a baking dish. Lay several large lumps of butter about it, and pour over a glassful of white wine or clear broth. Bake it in a moderate oven for half an hour—a large fish will take even longer. It should be basted frequently, being a dry fish. Good beef dripping will answer as well as butter. When done, lift the fish carefully on to a hot dish, and thicken the gravy with flour; add a spoonful of anchovy sauce, the same of mushroom ketchup, cayenne pepper, and salt. Let them boil up again, then stir in a spoonful of capers, and pour the sauce into a tureen. The fish may be garnished with horseradish, fresh parsley, or small ripe tomatoes, if available.

Pike may be boiled, letting it lie in vinegar some time previously, and placing it in very hot water or stock, with an onion and bunch of sweet herbs. Bring to a boil, and then simmer until tender. Serve it on a clean napkin with cut lemons and parsley; send a sharp sauce to table with it.

The remains of cold boiled pike, or slices cut from a fresh fish, may be dipped into egg and breadcrumbs and fried in fat. They will be found very good, especially if accompanied by a dish of green vegetable, as spinach, or a fresh salad.

Plaice.—Perhaps the very nicest way of dressing plaice is to cut the fish into fillets, then to dip these into beaten egg and raspings, and fry them. Place each fillet on a round of fried bread, and put a tiny pat of anchovy butter on the top of each, giving a sprinkle of pepper and salt as well, and thus they will be found to be very appetising.

Plaice, au Gratin.—Steep the fish in salt water for an hour or two, cleanse and empty it, leaving the head untouched. Dry it thoroughly, and take a dish that will just hold it. First melt a little beef dripping in that, then put a layer of crumbs, a tablespoonful of finely-minced suet, parsley, shallots, and seasoning. On this lay the plaice, white side uppermost, cover with the same order, and squeeze the juice of a lemon over the top. Set in the oven, which should be hot enough to brown the surface quickly. Twenty minutes is ample for a good-sized fish. Serve in the same dish.

Plaice, Boiled.—Large plaice should be chosen for boiling. Cut a slit from the head downwards through the middle of the back, to prevent the white side breaking. Lay it in the fish-kettle with sufficient *cold* water to cover it, and a teacupful of vinegar. Let it come quickly to boiling point, then simmer for about five minutes longer. Serve with shrimp or caper sauce.

Prawns.—Prawns much resemble shrimps, but are larger in size and more delicate in flavour. When fresh they are of a bright red colour, and very firm.

Prawn Soup.—Mince together till quite fine, a carrot, onion, stick of celery, and small turnip. Melt a little butter in a stewpan, put in the vegetables and let them simmer for a quarter of an hour, stirring well about. Heat a quart of clear stock, take a thick slice of white bread and cut it into dice, leaving out the crust, let it boil in the liquor, then add the vegetables with the butter, and a tablespoonful of salt. Boil all together. Take fifty prawns, pick out the tails, and stew the bodies in a glass of wine, press them through a colander and mix with the soup. Add then a pinch of cayenne pepper, a teaspoonful of anchovy butter, and a dessert-spoonful of lemon juice. Allow all to boil five minutes longer, and pour over fried croutons into a tureen.

Ray, or Maids.—This fish is the young skate, and, like the latter, it is improved by being hung for a day. It is nicest if cut into fillets and fried. It may be boiled for a few minutes in "court-bouillon," or, after being par- boiled, it may be cut into slices, dipped in oil, dredged with flour, and laid on a gridiron to broil for a few moments longer. Minced parsley and shallots simmered in butter, with a tablespoonful of vinegar, and seasoning of pepper and salt, should form a gravy to accompany the fillets.

Roach.—The roach is a small fresh-water fish of a firm compact flesh. It is best fried. Wash and empty the fish, dredge flour over them when dry, fry them in hot fat for about five minutes. Send anchovy or some very tasty sauce to table with them.

Salmon.—For boiling purposes choose salmon with small heads and thick shoulders, or if buying only a portion of a fish, choose a piece of the middle or the head and shoulders.

After cleaning the fish, cut off the fins and gills and scrape the scales carefully. Lay it in *nearly* boiling water with plenty of salt in it; let the water well cover the fish. Allow the water to come to boiling point, then boil gently until a silver fork will pass through the thickest part. As a general rule allow eight minutes to the pound if the fish is a thick one, five or six minutes if it be a thin one. Experience is the only safe guide. It is well to wrap the fish in a thin linen cloth before putting it in the pan; only be careful in removing the cloth when the fish is done, lest it be broken. Lay the fish on a folded napkin, and garnish with tufts of parsley, tomatoes, and a few prawns.

Salmon, Broiled.—For broiling purposes slices across the fish about an inch thick are preferable. If nicely cut and rubbed with a little melted butter, sprinkled with pepper and salt, laid on the gridiron and broiled on both sides over a very clear hot fire, turning every two or three minutes till done, then laid on a hot dish with a pat of fresh butter on each cutlet, and garnished with whatever is best obtainable, they are indeed truly admirable. Shrimp sauce, or *maître d'hôtel* butter might accompany them. A dish of green peas, either plainly boiled, or sautéd in butter, is a most delicious accompaniment to salmon cutlets.

Salmon, Baked.—Take a piece two or three pounds in weight, either from the middle or the tail end. Lay it in a deep pie-dish, surround it with a few small shallots and sound red tomatoes, dredge a little flour over it, sprinkle with pepper and salt, lay several small pats of butter on the top, and pour a glassful of white wine into the dish. Place the dish in a moderately hot oven and bake for from three-quarters to an hour. When done, lift the fish on to a dish and keep hot while preparing the sauce. Press the tomatoes and shallots through a colander or hair sieve, add to the liquor in the dish, with also a teaspoonful each of made mustard, vinegar, flour, and Worcestershire sauce; let this boil up once, then pour round the fish. Garnish with curled parsley and a few choice tomatoes. Serve whipped potatoes with it, and cucumbers sliced in vinegar.

Salmon Crumbs.—A dish much liked in the North of Ireland.

The remains of cold boiled salmon are divided into flakes and mixed with half their quantity of stale breadcrumbs, a tablespoonful of fresh butter, pepper, salt, a spoonful of vinegar, and one or two beaten eggs. Butter a shallow pie-dish, strew with crumbs, then press the mixture into it, and bake till brown. Any nice sauce, or a freshly-dressed salad, may be served with this dish.

Salmon Fritters.—Take the remains of cold cooked salmon, remove the skin and bone and break the flesh into flakes. Mix with these an equal quantity of mashed potatoes, add pepper and salt and an egg to bind the whole together. Make the mixture into small flat cakes or fritters, coat each one with beaten egg, and dredge with flour; melt a little nice dripping in a shallow frying-pan, fry the fritters first on one side, then on the other, till they are a nice brown colour, drain and keep hot while preparing the following:— The heart of a crisp white lettuce, shred, and piled in the centre of a dish, two hard-boiled eggs shelled and minced small, strewn over this; make a dressing with salt and pepper, one spoonful of vinegar and two of oil, the whole of a shallot, some chives and parsley finely minced, all mixed together, then poured over the lettuce. Sprinkle a little lobster coral over the surface, place the fritters round the base, and serve at once. This is a nice supper dish.

Salmon Trout.—These are rightly esteemed a great delicacy. They may be dressed and served according to the recipes given for salmon, although boiling is the least suitable method. As they seldom exceed two or three pounds in weight, it scarcely repays to fillet them. For broiling they may be treated like mackerel, but, better still, when they have been duly cleansed and scaled, wrap them in buttered paper, and either bake them in the oven or broil them on the gridiron. Baking is the best method of cooking salmon trout, but, when small, they are very good if dipped bodily into batter, then plunged into boiling fat, and served with *maître d'hôtel* sauce.

Salmon Trout, Baked and Stuffed.—A good-sized trout is very nice if baked as follows:—After emptying and scaling the fish, fill the cavity with a stuffing of breadcrumbs, parsley, herbs, and an egg to mix it; sew the sides together if necessary. Lay in a baking dish, dredge with flour, place butter on the top, put a tablespoonful of vinegar and one of stock into the dish, and bake in the oven from twenty minutes to half an hour. Lift the fish out on to a dish, thicken the liquor with flour, add seasoning, a spoonful of chopped parsley, a teaspoonful of anchovy essence, and pour this sauce round the fish. New potatoes, green peas, or baked tomatoes should accompany this dish.

Sardines.—Tinned sardines are generally eaten without any further preparation, although very nice sandwiches may be made from them, also they are an indispensable adjunct to a fish salad.

Fresh sardines should be first cleansed, then dried in a soft cloth, laid on the gridiron and broiled for about two minutes. Sprinkle salt and pepper and a dash of vinegar over them, and serve very hot on toasted bread.

Shad.—Shad does not enjoy a very high reputation in England; in France it is quite a favourite fish and is thought worthy of being cooked in wine, and served with Béchamel sauce. Its best season is the early spring- time, March to May. The French way of cooking it is to split it open, after emptying, scaling, and washing it, then to lay it in oil, with pepper and salt. After it has soaked in this marinade for a sufficient time, it is laid on the gridiron, and broiled *very slowly*, on both sides, for upwards of an hour. Served with *maître d'hôtel* butter or caper sauce. Shad may be fried after first trimming into convenient-sized pieces and dipping each piece in frying batter. It may also be stuffed and baked according to instructions given for salmon trout.

Shrimps.—There are several varieties of shrimps. The two kinds most commonly met with are the brown and the red shrimps. The brown kind is caught nearest to the shore in the shallower pools, and has the strongest flavour. The red shrimp is generally much smaller in size and more refined in flavour. When freshly boiled, shrimps are excellent as a breakfast relish, but when stale they are far from wholesome. Allow a good handful of coarse salt to the quart of water when boiling; as soon as they have attained a nice colour they are done.

Shrimps, Potted.—In potting shrimps, after they have been well boiled, take care to pick off both heads and tails and to twist them dexterously out of the shells. As a good quantity of shrimps are required to make a small amount, it is as well to benefit by an opportunity of shrimp sauce being required, and so set aside the heads and tails to be used for the latter purpose. After having thoroughly pounded the bodies of the shrimps in a mortar, put in a small saltspoonful of salt and the same of pepper, and one or two ounces of fresh butter. Pound all well together, press into small pots, and pour clarified butter on the surface to exclude the air.

Shrimp butter is made in the same way, only adding an *equal* quantity of butter to the paste. Neither of these will keep good many days.

Shrimp Forcemeat, for stuffing sea or fresh-water fish.

Shred some shrimps and add to them an equal quantity of fresh breadcrumbs. To a tablespoonful of fresh butter add a saltspoonful of seasoning, and a beaten egg. Make the shrimps and crumbs into a stiff paste with this. Particularly good as a forcemeat for pike and carp.

Shrimp Patties.—(The same mixture is used for shrimp "vol-au-vent"). Pick off the heads and tails from freshly-boiled shrimps, and shell them. Put the shells into a saucepan, cover them with water, and boil gently for a quarter of an hour. Strain the liquor, then thicken it with a teaspoonful of arrowroot, add the yolk of an egg, salt and pepper to taste, a small nob of butter, stir all together over the fire; when it is of the consistency of cream, put in the bodies of the shrimps to heat through and draw the saucepan to one side until required. Make some good puff paste, line the patty pans, and put a morsel of soft bread in the middle before putting on the cover. Bake the patties to a nice brown, then remove the bread, replacing it with a spoonful of the mixture, put on the cover, brush over the surface and edges with beaten yolk of egg and water, return the patties to the oven to heat them through again, then send to table on a pretty d'oyley. They are very good also for eating cold. If liked, the top crust may be omitted, and a few breadcrumbs be sprinkled over the top of the mixture. Garnish the dish with curly parsley and a few large shrimps.

Shrimp Canapés.—A nice entrée. Cut some small rounds from a stale loaf of bread, fry them in oil or lard to a delicate brown, then cover each with a layer of either potted shrimps or shrimp butter. Hard boil two eggs. Remove the yolks, and pound them with a small bit of butter and a pinch of pepper and salt. Cut the whites into thin strips. Lay the strips in a lattice work over the rounds and place a pat of the yellow mixture in the middle of them, and a whole shrimp on that, or the very tiniest sprig of parsley. Make a bed of fresh dry parsley on a dish to lay the rounds upon.

Skate.—Skate is an unwholesome fish if eaten out of season. Its best time is during the winter months, and it is positively improved by being kept for a day or two hung up. However it is dressed it should always be skinned first. The liver is a choice morsel.

A method of dressing skate which is much liked by French people, is to do it *à la Sainte Ménehould.* For this it should be skinned and cut into neat pieces, then simmered in white sauce till tender; the pieces of fish should then be lifted out on to a shallow dish, the sauce to receive the addition of a yolk of egg and pinch of cayenne pepper, then to be poured over the fish, Parmesan or Cheshire cheese grated over the top. Set the dish in the oven to get thoroughly hot again.

For boiling, large skate are preferable to small ones, and when possible they should be crimped. (N.B.—Crimping can only be done when the fish is perfectly fresh.) It should be plunged into boiling salt water, then gently simmered till tender. Let it drain well.

Boiled skate is very good served with "Black Butter" sauce. For this last, a quarter pound of butter should be allowed to frizzle in a saucepan until of a light brown colour, then a few washed and dried parsley leaves should be thrown in, a tablespoonful of tarragon vinegar, ditto of mushroom ketchup, Worcestershire sauce, and chopped capers, pepper and salt to taste. Let these boil once, then either pour over the fish or send to table in a tureen.

Skate may also be fried, curried, or stewed, according to directions given for other fish.

Smelts.—Smelts should be handled as little as possible; not washed, but wiped with a cloth. The inside should be pulled out with the gills, as they must not be opened.

It is most usual to fry smelts. Boiling is not to be recommended, unless for an invalid, in which case they should be put into boiling water which contains a few parsley leaves and a lump or two of sugar as well as salt; four minutes cooking is ample time. A little of the liquor in which they were boiled should receive the addition of cream and chopped parsley, and be served with them.

For frying, smelts should be first dipped into beaten egg, then into mixed flour and breadcrumbs, afterwards fried in a good depth of boiling fat. Lift them out with a slice, drain well, and garnish with cut lemon.

Smelts are delicious as a breakfast relish if laid on a gridiron and broiled lightly on both sides, then placed on a hot dish, sprinkled with pepper and salt, lemon juice squeezed over, and a pat of butter placed on each.

They may also be baked *au gratin*, and served in the same dish.

Soles.—The popular method of cooking this favourite fish is to fry them. Some persons declare it to be the best method. If it be so or not, certain it is that the following ways, when fairly tried, will be found to compete very closely in favour. *Very* large soles may be boiled whole, and will be found most agreeable eating, not unlike turbot in flavour. When practicable, soles should be cleansed a couple of hours before they are wanted for cooking, wrapped in a towel and laid in a cool place to stiffen. The fishmonger will generally skin them; if not, it is easy to draw the skin off the back beginning at the head, gut them, and take out the roe, if any.

Soles, Fried.—Medium sized fish are the best for frying whole, or if large they should be filleted. After cleansing them be careful to wipe *very* dry, then dip them first into flour, next into beaten egg, and cover with bread raspings. Fry quickly in plenty of boiling fat. From five to ten minutes is the time a moderate sized sole will require—but when of a rich colour it is generally cooked sufficiently. Lay on a wire sieve or blotting-paper to drain before putting on to a dish. Garnish with cut lemons and parsley, either fresh or fried.

Sole, Boiled.—Let the sole be large, thick, and firm; it should not weigh less than two pounds. Wrap it in a clean white cloth (a napkin which is too old for table use is best), plunge it into boiling salted water with a tablespoonful of vinegar, let it boil very gently for about seven or eight minutes, according to size, then drain well, lay carefully on a clean napkin. Garnish with sliced tomatoes and lemons, and tufts of parsley. Send to table either melted butter, shrimp, or anchovy sauce.

Soles, Baked au Gratin.—Melt an ounce of butter in a gratin-dish, or tin baking dish. Chop finely two or three shallots, a small bunch of parsley, and few herbs, grate a slice of stale bread. Sprinkle half the quantity of these at the bottom of the dish, lay the sole upon that and cover with the remainder. Pour either a glass of white wine or the juice of a lemon over all, lay a few bits of butter at the top, and bake in a quick oven for twenty minutes. Serve in the same dish, sprinkled with salt and pepper. Or soles are very nice if laid in a buttered dish, having rubbed them with flour, more butter placed on the top, and baked till lightly browned. They may be lifted on to another dish, but the butter should be served with them.

Sole à la Normande.—This is an epicure's dish. After skinning and cleaning a large sole, dry it thoroughly and rub with flour. Take a gratin-dish, or a porcelain one which will stand fire. Slice two shallots very thinly, brown them in butter, and lay at the bottom of the dish with more butter. Lay the sole in the dish, sprinkle it with salt and pepper, and cover with a glass of white wine. Bake in a gentle oven until tender through. Meanwhile make some rich white sauce with cream; if possible, take a few oysters, beard them, and put them into the sauce with their liquor; let the sauce merely simmer after this. Open a small tin of button mushrooms, mince them finely, and strew them over the sole, let them get hot through, then pour the oyster sauce over all. Garnish with a few shrimps, and place tiny croutons of fried bread round the edge.

Cider may be used instead of wine.

Soles, Filleted.—Fillet a large sole by slitting it down the middle of the back, and with a sharp knife raising the flesh from the bone on each side. Divide the meat into convenient sized pieces, say two inches broad and three long, make a marinade of salt, pepper, vinegar, and oil, lay the fillets in this, turning them often, and let them lie an hour or so. Prepare a frying batter—a heaped spoonful of flour mixed smooth with a little oil and cold water, a pinch of salt, and the whites of two eggs—it should be fairly thick. Well coat each fillet with this, then drop into boiling fat, and fry till a nice brown. Garnish prettily, and serve with tomato sauce.

The fillets of sole may be dipped into egg and bread raspings, fried, then laid in the following sauce to heat through, before serving altogether: half a pint of clear stock thickened with a tablespoonful of flour, mixed smooth with butter, a tablespoonful of mushroom ketchup, a teaspoonful of curry powder, the same of tarragon vinegar, and a pinch of salt. Let the sauce be well cooked before putting in the fillets.

The fillets, or small soles whole, may be gently simmered in butter till tender, then laid on a hot dish, and white sauce seasoned with salt, pepper, and lemon juice, be poured over them. If the soles be *boiled* for two minutes only before putting them in the butter, and the sauce be made with cream, this will be found a most delicious way of dressing them for invalids.

Sprats.—Sprats resemble herrings very closely. They are abundant on the North British coasts, particularly in the Firth of Forth. In Edinburgh and Glasgow they are known as "garvies." They may be cooked in any of the ways prescribed for herrings, but are best broiled over the fire, and lemon juice improves the flavour of them.

Sturgeon.—The sturgeon is somewhat of a rarity in English markets, although common enough in Russia. It is regarded as a royal fish, and is proportionately costly. Its flesh is delicious, and the caviare which the Russians prepare from the roe is justly esteemed a great delicacy.

The Russian method of dressing it is to par-boil it in water with onions, herbs, and baysalt, then to drain it, dredge it with flour, and pour melted butter liberally over it, then to lay it before a bright fire to roast, serving with a rich sauce, either poured over it, or in a tureen.

Sturgeon is very good if simply roasted before the fire, taking care to baste frequently with butter. Of course all the skin and spikes are previously stripped off, and the fish well cleansed.

Sturgeon, Stewed.—This is one of the best ways of cooking a portion of this fish. Take two or three slices about an inch thick, let them steep in vinegar awhile. Dry them, dip in flour, and place in some frothing butter in a covered stewpan. Let them brown on both sides, then remove the fish, and in its place put a few shallots, half a small carrot cut into dice, and some button mushrooms. When these have browned, cover them with half a pint of clear veal broth, a good tumblerful of claret, a teaspoonful of salt and pepper mixed, then replace the slices of sturgeon. Let all stew together for upwards of an hour, when remove the fish on to a dish, strain the sauce from the vegetables, thicken it with a little flour rolled in butter, and add a spoonful of some sharp sauce. Pour over the fish on the dish.

Tench.—River tench are the best for the table. They somewhat resemble carp, but are smaller in size and of a richer flavour. They should lie in salt water for a few hours, then be turned into clear spring water, to rid them of the slight muddy flavour which they are apt to have. The cold winter months are their best season.

Empty and scale the tench very carefully, always removing the gills, as they are most apt to retain the muddy flavour. After the fish is cleansed it is a good plan to rub it well over with lemon juice. It may then be baked *au gratin*, or boiled in salt water, or broiled over the fire. If the last-named method be chosen, let the fish be steeped in oil, sprinkled with salt and pepper, and wrapped in oiled paper before laying on the gridiron. Great care is needed not to let the paper catch fire. Remove the paper before bringing to table, lay the fish on a hot dish and serve a *sauce piquante* over it.

The time it takes to cook will depend entirely on the size of the fish. Broiling will require about ten minutes to the pound; boiling and baking rather less time.

Tench is also good if fried. After scaling and cleaning it should be dipped into vinegar and water, dried, and split open; dredge it with flour, and plunge into boiling fat. Serve garnished with parsley and lemons.

Trout, Baked.—One of the nicest ways of dressing trout is to simply bake them with butter. Wash, empty, and dry the trout, sprinkle them with seasoned flour, lay in a baking tin in which a little butter has been melted, place several pats of butter over them, and bake about twenty minutes. Lift them out on to a dish, garnish with parsley, thicken the butter slightly, stir in a spoonful of chopped parsley and a squeeze of lemon juice, and pour the sauce round the fish.

Trout, Boiled.—Fresh trout is excellent if boiled in "court- bouillon" for ten to fifteen minutes, then drained and served with Dutch sauce or melted butter. This method is similar to that recommended by the great

Izaak Walton.

Turbot.—The turbot is the king of flat fish, and is justly held in high estimation. It is rather an expensive fish, and is mostly sold by size. At its best from February to August. It will keep good for a day, or even two, if slightly salted. Salt should be rubbed all over to help to remove the slime. The fins should not be cut off, but an incision should be made all the way down the middle of the backbone on the *dark* side to prevent the white side cracking. Lemon juice rubbed over it helps to preserve the colour. Any unsightly spots on the white side may be removed by rubbing with salt and lemon juice.

Turbot, Boiled.—After preparing the turbot according to the directions given above, lay it in the turbot kettle and cover with cold water to the depth of an inch. Allow a good handful of salt to a gallon of water. Bring it up to boiling point as quickly as possible, and remove the scum as it rises. When it boils draw it aside to simmer gently, watch it carefully, and as soon as it shows signs of the flesh shrinking from the bone, lift it out on the drainer, let it drain a minute, then slide it carefully on to a clean napkin. Garnish with parsley, cut lemons, and if a few crayfish are obtainable they add greatly to the beauty of the dish. A sprinkling of lobster coral on the white surface is very pretty.

Whatever sauce accompanies boiled turbot, it should be brought to table in a tureen.

A pretty way of garnishing boiled turbot in summer time is to surround it with a border of nasturtium flowers.

Turbot, with Anchovy Cream.—Boil a medium sized turbot according to the last recipe—by the way, a turbot ought to be thick and of a creamy white colour; if thin and bluish looking it is not a good one. Lay the fish on a hot dish without a napkin, cover to keep it hot. Then into half a pint of plain melted butter, stir in a good teaspoonful of essence of anchovies, and a quarter of a pint of rich cream; let it nearly boil, then pour over the turbot. Chop small a few pickled gherkins and capers, strew them over the surface. Before bringing to table, make a border round this of new kidney potatoes, well boiled but not broken; garnish the outer edge with parsley.

Turbot à la Béchamel.—This is one of the best ways of dressing cold turbot. Make a pint of Béchamel sauce by boiling together equal quantities of good white stock and cream in an enamelled saucepan, also a strip of fresh lemon rind and two or three shallots. Add a mixed teaspoonful of salt and pepper, thicken with a spoonful of arrowroot, and let it boil well.

Remove the lemon rind and shallots, and put in the pieces of turbot to heat through, all skin and bone removed. When quite hot, pour all together on to a hot dish; if liked, a few oysters may be added to the sauce just before turning it out. Some potato croquettes are a nice addition to this dish.

Turbot Salad.—The remains of cold turbot will make an excellent salad. Free it from all skin and bone, and divide into pieces about an inch square. Sprinkle the pieces with salt and pepper and a little vinegar. Take two large fresh lettuces, let them be quite clean and dry. Make a dressing for the salad of the beaten yolks of two eggs, a teaspoonful of made mustard, salt and pepper, four spoonsful of oil, and one of tarragon vinegar. Arrange the salad in a bowl or dish by making a layer of shred lettuce leaves, then one of fish, and a few spoonsful of the dressing, and continue thus until the material is used up. Garnish the top with sliced beetroot, hard-boiled eggs, &c., and let the salad stand in a cold place for half an hour.

Turbot may be cooked *au gratin* if of a small size, allowing white wine or cider to it. French cooks generally prefer to par-boil it in "court-bouillon," then to take it out and finish cooking it in white sauce.

Whitebait.—Whitebait are genuine Cockney fish, being found alone in the Thames in perfection. They make their appearance early in the year, but the season *par excellence* is the month of May. They cannot be had too fresh; if not used instantly they are brought in, they should lie in ice-water until required.

It is generally thought that only a "professional" can cook whitebait, but if due care be given there is no reason why they should be beyond the skill of the amateur. The principal thing to observe is the *drying* of the fish. After well draining them they should be thrown on to a floured cloth—a cloth containing flour an inch in depth. When thus dosed, the fish should be put into a sifter and lightly shaken to remove all superfluous flour. They should next be put into a wire basket, a few at a time, and plunged into a pan containing a good depth of boiling fat. A minute generally suffices to cook them, then they should be laid on a hot dish, garnished with fried parsley, and sent to table instantly. It is absolutely needful to fry the whitebait the moment after it is floured; if allowed to remain on one side for only a few minutes, it becomes flabby and spoilt. Thin brown bread and butter and slices of lemon are an indispensable accompaniment to whitebait. For "Devilled Whitebait" lift out the basket of fish when only half cooked, pepper them with black or cayenne pepper and return to the fat to finish cooking.

Whiting.—Whiting are excellent fish when fresh, the flesh being light, tender, and easy of digestion. The firmness of the flesh, and its silvery hue, are the signs by which to judge of its freshness. It is more or less in season all the year, but at its best in the winter months. Occasionally they attain to a considerable size, but are mostly from one to two pounds in weight. Those about nine inches in length are the best in point of flavour.

Whiting are best broiled or fried.

Whiting, Broiled.—Wash in salted water, split them open, and dry thoroughly. Dip them in oil, sprinkle with seasoning, dredge with flour, and then lay on a greased gridiron, and broil lightly on both sides. Place them on a hot dish, put a pat of butter on each, and serve smoking hot.

Whiting, Fried.—Empty, and wash the fish, skin it, and then draw the tail through the mouth. Dip each one first into flour, then in beaten egg and breadcrumbs, drop into boiling fat, and fry to a golden brown. Garnish the dish with fried parsley, and send sauce to table in a tureen.

A large whiting may be split open, floured, and then fried in a smaller quantity of fat. When done, lay it on a dish and pour the following sauce over it: A tablespoonful of minced herbs, the same of parsley, a pinch of seasoning, an ounce of fresh butter, and small glass of white wine all boiled together.

PART IV.

FISH SAUCES.

A few plain directions as to the making of sauces suitable for serving with fish, will, we think, not be unwelcome. First as to that sauce commonly known as—

Melted Butter.—In France this sauce is what its name declares it to be, viz., a tureen half full of pure butter dissolved, in strong contrast to that generally found on English tables, where a mixture of milk and water thickened with flour, is usually dignified with this title. True "butter sauce" belongs to neither of these extremes. As one ladleful will generally suffice for each individual partaking of fish, it is as well to measure into the saucepan the number of ladlefuls that will be required, so that there shall be no waste of good material.

Having ascertained how much liquid will be in the saucepan when the sauce is finished, pour away the water and proceed to divide the materials you will use. A small lump of butter should be allowed for each ladleful of sauce. Take one lump and let it dissolve, then stir in a heaped tablespoonful of dry flour, mix these quite smoothly together, with the addition of cold water, until like a cream; add boiling water to make half the quantity of sauce, then stir in by degrees the remaining lumps of butter. If the sauce shows signs of looking oily, a little cold water will correct it. A pinch of salt should be added, or salt butter may be used.

Maître d'Hôtel Butter.—For this prepare a little melted butter, by mixing an ounce of butter with the same weight of flour, and cold water to make it smooth. Dilute with a quarter of a pint of white stock. Let this mixture boil, then stir in a tablespoonful of chopped parsley, one of sweet herbs, half one of minced chives, a teaspoonful of mixed salt and pepper, the juice of a lemon, or a spoonful of tarragon vinegar, and a spoonful of pure oil; when these have been well mixed together, draw aside the saucepan and stir in the beaten yolk of an egg, then pour into a hot tureen.

Herb Sauce: for Broiled Fish.—Chop some dry parsley until quite fine, also an equal quantity of mixed herbs—thyme, marjoram, sage, chervil, celery, fennel, &c. Put first a small lump of butter to dissolve in the saucepan, and chop finely a shallot and let it frizzle in this, then stir in the parsley and herbs, and add sufficient vinegar to cover them. Draw the saucepan aside and let it simmer ten minutes to abstract the flavour. Just before it is wanted, add pepper and a pinch of salt, also a good tablespoonful of oil. A yolk of egg, added lastly, will slightly thicken and improve it, but it is very good without, especially for broiled herrings and mackerel.

Anchovy Sauce.—Anchovy sauce is quickly and easily made according to the recipe given in the previous chapter (see letter A), but if a richer sauce is desired, the anchovies should be boiled gently until they dissolve. Then the liquor be strained, added to a little plain melted butter with a glass of port wine.

Shrimp Sauce.—For this the foundation is again "melted butter," and to half a pint of that allow half a pint of shrimps. Pick off heads, tails, and shells, and let the bodies stew gently in the sauce, but not boil, or they will harden. Add a pinch of cayenne pepper, a little lemon-juice, a drop of anchovy essence, and salt to taste.

Lobster Sauce can be made in the same way, using a little of the white meat of the lobster torn into flakes, in place of the shrimps, and stirring in a spoonful of lobster butter. It must not boil or the colour will be spoilt. To give this sauce a stronger flavour of lobster, the shell may be boiled in water, and the liquor used instead of water.

Fennel Sauce.—Pick some fennel from the stalk and boil it for a minute, then chop it fine and add to some "melted butter." Stir in the yolk of an egg the last thing. A teaspoonful of spiced vinegar will give piquancy to it.

Parsley Sauce.—Parsley sauce is merely "melted butter" with chopped parsley stirred in. It is an improvement to let the sauce boil a moment or two after to take off the raw flavour.

Horseradish Sauce.—To two tablespoonsful of finely-scraped horseradish and one of stale white breadcrumbs allow half a pint of cream—or new milk and cream—and a pinch of salt. Let this stew for fifteen minutes, then stir in a spoonful of vinegar just before serving.

Gooseberry Sauce, for Mackerel.—Stew half a pint of gooseberries in a little water until very soft, press them through a sieve into the same quantity of "melted butter," add an ounce of white sugar, and a spoonful of spinach-juice to give a nice green colour.

Egg Sauce.—*First Way:* Make some good "melted butter," stir into it two or three hard-boiled eggs which have been cut up small, and season it well. Just before serving stir in the beaten yolk of a fresh egg.

Second Way (for cold fish): Beat the yolks of two fresh eggs, stir in a teaspoonful of made mustard, half a teaspoonful of mixed salt and pepper, and by degrees two tablespoonsful of salad oil and one of tarragon vinegar. It should be of the consistency of cream. This sauce is almost identical with "Mayonnaise" sauce, and to make a green mayonnaise add finely-minced chives, parsley, chervil, and cress.

Tomato Sauce.—Melt an ounce of butter, and slice one or two tomatoes thinly into it, add one or two shallots. Let these stew till quite soft, then press through a wire sieve. Add a little more butter to this purée, plenty of salt and pepper, and a spoonful of vinegar. Make thoroughly hot before serving.

Regard should always be had to contrast of colour in garnishing all dishes. Where the fish is masked in white sauce, the introduction of something red amongst the green garnishing is a relief to the eye. Flowers may be used to supply this needful touch of colour, slices of beetroot, or a few strips of boiled carrot, or a few bright prawns, one or two chilies, &c.

If a portion of salmon, showing the bright colour of the meat, is the dish which has to be trimmed, a few mounds of scraped horseradish alternating with tufts of curly parsley looks well.

For fried fish—soles, fillets, lobster cutlets, &c., it is better to fry the parsley which is used for their garnishing. Double-curled parsley, well dried, thrown into a wire basket and plunged into the boiling fat, for one minute only, is the way to obtain this.

Crisp, fried croutons of bread, tiny potato balls, rice balls, sliced lemons, small bright tomatoes, and slices of hard-boiled egg, are all excellent for garnishing purposes.

Fish that has been baked in the oven—excepting always that which has been done *au gratin*, and which requires no garnish—will often be made to look very pretty if a few fancy shapes be stamped out of cooked vegetables, say the red of a carrot, the white of a turnip, tiny sprigs of cauliflower, &c., always using green parsley to finish off the outer edge. Where there is the will to do it, means will not be lacking whereby the simplest dish may be made to look elegant.

The Gresham Press,

UNWIN BROTHERS

WOKING AND LONDON.